1

HOW TO WRITE AN EBOOK

How to write an e-book

Claude HAJOS

3

Translated from the French book by Claude HAJOS

By the same author in English

- How to write a play

- How to write a screenplay

- How to write your autobiography

- How to write a biography

- Sell luxury real estate

- Winning Poker – The Real Method

- The solution to all your problems

- Autobiography - Biography

- Theater play – Film script

- How to write an ebook

By the same author in French

- Comment écrire un roman
- Comment écrire un ebook
- Comment écrire un article
- Comment écrire une nouvelle
- Comment écrire une pièce de théâtre
- Comment écrire un scénario
- Comment écrire son autobiographie
- Comment écrire une biographie

- Les erreurs dans l'immobilier – Les erreurs des acheteurs, des vendeurs et des professionnels
- Formation promotion immobilière – Stratégie pour se lancer dans la promotion immobilière
- Formation commerciale conseil en gestion de patrimoine
- Formation commerciale pour agents, négociateurs et mandataires en immobilier
- Comment bien choisir son réseau de mandataires
- Cinq méthodes pour booster votre activité de CGP
- Vendre de l'immobilier de prestige

- Comment booster votre activité d'agent, de négociateur ou de mandataire en immobilier
- Construire sa maison – Le guide pratique
- La vente en VEFA – Stratégie pour vendre de l'immobilier neuf
- Comment créer sa propre agence immobilière
- 52 exercices pour devenir le n°1 de l'immobilier
- LA formation immobilière – Stratégie avec exercice

ROMANS ET FICTIONS

- Le Politicard tome 1 (*Les aventures complètement loufoques de Coco Chanoune*)
- Le Politicard tome 2 (*Y a-t-il un candidat dans la salle ?*)
- Le Politicard tome 3 (*Recherche Modjo désespérément*)
- Le Politicard tome 4 (*Vos gueules les mouettes !*)
- Le Politicard tome 5 (*Chaud devant à Brégançon*)
- Le Politicard tome 6 (*Boycott*)
- Le Politicard tome 7 (*Madame Irma*)
- Le Politicard tome 8 (*Bakchich*)
- J'aime tous les Juifs sauf ma mère...
- Deux pieds dans la chambre, un pied dans la tombe tome 1 (*Le contrat*)
- Deux pieds dans la chambre, un pied dans la tombe tome 2 (*L'exécution*)
- Deux pieds dans la chambre, un pied dans la tombe tome 3 (*Coup de théâtre*)
- Meurtres au Club Med tome 1 (*Macabre découverte*)
- Meurtres au Club Med tome 2 (*Panique à bord*)
- Meurtres au Club Med tome 3 (*Investigations*)
- Les gogos tome 1 (*Limit-up & limit-down*)
- Les gogos tome 2 (*Appel de marge*)
- Les gogos tome 3 (*Cash*)
- Comment arrondir ses fins de mois volume 1
- Comment arrondir ses fins de mois volume 2
- Comment arrondir ses fins de mois volume 3
- Les chroniques de Raoul volume 1
- Les chroniques de Raoul volume 2
- Les chroniques de Raoul volume 3
- Les chroniques de Raoul volume 4

- Poker gagnant – La vraie méthode
- La solution à tous vos problèmes

Préamble

Since the advent of the internet and it is obvious, the digital book is developing more and more, to the detriment of the paper book.

Thus, in certain countries such as Japan and South Korea, to name only these two, at the beginning of their schooling, schoolchildren use computers and digital tablets from an early age to abandon of course paper as we still know it.

All countries are also gradually going digital and even if as far as we are concerned, paper certainly has a bright future ahead of it, the question is how long will it last.

Because you can't fight against progress, even if there were always some irreducible defenders of paperback books.

To be convinced of this, it suffices to refer to past history to understand, and it is only pure evidence, that at one time or another, the sale of books in digital format will catch up with and exceed that of books in paper format.

Moreover, this is already the case in Japan, Korea, the United States and in quite a few other countries.

This will also be the case with us, probably within the next 5 to 10 years.

So why not prepare to publish directly digitally in PDF format, without going through the paper version ?

Because if the paper still offers advantages in the eyes of some, they do not weigh very heavy compared to the advantages of digital.

In fact, the only argument of the defenders of the paper is the touch.

The touch of paper... But still, it's not just that...

There is the feeling that one can have when one leafs through the pages of a book...

Also the pleasure that can be experienced by highlighting it in a library or on a shelf...

Not to mention the very practical gift to offer, both to children and adults...

In short, so many satisfactions that can objectively justify the possession of this kind of work, to the delight of all fans.

*

*   *

It is well known that in France there is always a little resistance when it comes to dealing with changes.

It is part of our culture and our temperament.

We are all more or less resistant to progress, especially when it leads to profound changes in our way of life and our ways of doing things.

Because in truth, if Gutenberg upset his time by creating a new form of printing, internet and digital are not left out.

And unless we want to put up front resistance, we won't escape it.

Because in reality, digital also offers a lot of advantages and if the Americans, the Japanese, the Koreans, the Chinese, the Indians and many other countries are getting into it, it is probably not by chance, nor on a whim.

Basically and to simplify, with digital, we will save entire forests of trees intended to be felled to make paper.

Saving entire forests means more oxygen, it means less pollution, it means things are going in the right direction.

But it's not just that...

In digital format, it is possible to download them either on computers or tablets, but also on e-readers, so practical when you have tried them at least once.

A reading light can store several hundred books at the same time.

You can read them anytime, in any light, because the latest models have improved so much over the previous ones that it's a bit like night and day.

In addition, it is a light device, much lighter than a book and therefore easier to carry.

*

*   *

Publishing digitally is like typing text directly from a keyboard. So forget the paper and long live the screen !

Now, I can perfectly understand that this could put off more than one person but hey, everyone is free to position themselves as they wish.

So anyway, if you choose to publish your books directly digitally, the first piece of advice I can give you is to practice typing or typing as quickly as possible, without having to take both of you back words.

Typing quickly will allow you to better stay focused on your subject and therefore gain in efficiency.

Because if it's to go much slower than writing on paper with a pen or a quill, there's no point.

The interest of publishing in e-book, via digital, is mainly based on two fundamental notions.

On the one hand, speed. But that we just talked about.

On the other hand, the content of the e-book and the way to transcribe it.

And this is precisely the subject of this book, especially since the publication in digital form, I know well.

*

*   *

If you have followed my previous training, writing an e-book should not be a problem for you.

So what content will you find in this book? Simply everything that has not yet been said about digital books in particular!

Everything you think you know.

And everything you don't know.

1 - Important

Before getting to the heart of the matter, just a quick note.

I very regularly see manuals on writing digital books.

According to the authors, nothing would be easier than writing an e-book and for that, they make a point of explaining how to do it.

It would be enough to meet people's expectations.

So if it was just that, I agree, it could be easy.

Except that it is absolutely nothing !

First of all, what does it mean to meet people's expectations ?

It simply means that there are people who are looking for solutions, to solve some of their problems.

Moreover, in all these e-books where we are taught to write, we are regularly harped on the eternal truth, namely that we must find solutions to people's problems.

Which means two things in particular.

■ **Either you have already experienced this kind of very specific problem and you were able to remedy it**.

And from your own experience, you try to share it in a way that it can benefit others.

So in this case, yes why not, because you embody a certain legitimacy in the sense that you know your subject for having experienced it.

Now, everyone knows that the solutions of some are not necessarily the solutions of others.

But still, when you derive legitimacy in any area, you can and have the right to share it.

■ **Either you have never experienced this kind of very specific problem and therefore you have nothing to offer personally, for lack of having experienced anything**.

And this is precisely where the problem lies, because in all these training courses intended to write an e-book, we are clearly told that there is no need to be a specialist in anything to be able to write about everything.

From there, everything is said !

Because between us...

How can you claim to be relevant about something you know nothing about ?

How do you want to share an inexperience with people who live their problem on a daily basis, without you yourself having the slightest idea, for lack of having experienced the same thing ?

No, let's be serious anyway.

If you want to start publishing one or more e-books, you must know your subject well.

That's the first thing to consider.

Because apart from talking about rain or shine and engaging in trade show conversations, when people buy an e-book on a very specific problem, you have to know how to talk about it.

It's still a minimum.

*
*   *

2 – Knowledge and skills

From there, here's what to do. List precisely on a sheet of paper or on an Excel table whatever your areas of expertise are.

I am talking about skill areas.

No knowledge.

Because if knowledge is one thing, competence is another.

▶ For example, you can know the dogs because from time to time, you happen to pet one or even make him sit down and ask him for the paw while dangling a cake to him, so that he listens to you better.

It is a certain form of knowledge, based on your own knowledge and your own appreciation, according to your personal experience. On the other hand, from there, can you reasonably and irrefutably claim that you are competent in dog training ?

Because between the two, there is a whole world.

So if in this spirit, you would have been tempted to tick competent in matters of dogs, forget very quickly because you will certainly not be able to meet the needs of your readers, who are looking for solutions to educate their animal.

What I want to tell you is that when we look at this subject, that is to say the notion of competence, the minimum of intellectual honesty is to recognize one's limits and to stay on what you know how to do well or in any case, do better.

And you'll see very quickly that even if you look hard enough, you'll have a hard time listing as many skills as the fingers of one hand.

Now don't confuse competence with having a taste for certain things.

As short as your list of skills will be, a list of tastes for certain things can be endlessly long.

For example, one can be competent in something very specific, cooking why not and love cars, football, TV, beer, tennis, scrabble, paragliding, guitar, classical music, jazz , the countryside, skiing, the sea, trucks, grasshoppers, cinema, elephants, chocolate mousse, pasta, theatre, table tennis, perfumes, wine, fast food, starred restaurants, champagne, flowers, lakes and rivers, fishing, hunting, bungee jumping, cart racing, etc.

As much as writing and publishing e-books dealing with cooking and its different approaches and everything that can revolve around it will be perfectly legitimate, as much as writing and publishing e-books on everything else will be another thing.

*
*　*

3 – Meet a need

We have seen previously that when we write e-books, it is to meet a need.

Because we are not in a logic to write a novel or an autobiography, ie a fiction or a part of yourself, but to write a manual intended to find solutions to solve problems.

So yes, when you are competent in a certain discipline, it will necessarily be very easy to talk about it, to deliver anecdotes, to entrust certain little manufacturing secrets, to tell their origin and their brief history, to interest your readers and make them want to follow you.

Because in reality, this is exactly what your readers are looking for. They want concrete. They want examples. They want you to tell them about your own experience. Above all, they want the solutions you have in place to remedy all your problems.

While if you don't have any particular skill but just more or less precise, more or less vague knowledge, how do you want to interest them, except to fill in pages of useless spiel.

*

*   *

4 – Intentions

After determining which areas of expertise you can build on, think about your intentions.

Maybe you only plan to write and publish one e-book, with no preconceived ideas afterwards.

But perhaps you already have an idea in mind, that of setting up a collection in your chosen field and why not, in this logic, of writing ten or twenty books and even more, in which case it will You have to seriously think about it before you start.

I will give you a very personal example.

Before I started writing articles for the Raoul du Tonnerre de Dieu series (I wrote nearly a hundred) I asked myself the question of knowing, on the one hand, what could well connect me in this way and on the other hand, if I would be able to write as many as I would like.

And that's what led me to choose a theme based on what I called annoying questions, treated with a certain amount of humor and above all not taken literally.

This kind of article doesn't take me more than an hour and I could probably write a lot more.

Another very personal example.

I also started writing short stories, still under the pseudonym of Raoul du Tonnerre de Dieu.

Today, I have written more than fifteen.

Before I get started, I have a theme to build on.

This is how I found material by proposing ideas to improve its end of the month.

Until then, nothing very original because ideas to improve your end of the month, you can find them everywhere.

Except that there, it is about new ideas and for the less unusual and expressed with great reinforcement of humor.

In short, not to be taken at face value !

(For example : how to make ends meet by becoming a kidnapper, how to make ends meet by becoming a hitman, how to make ends meet by robbing an armored car, etc.)

As I told you, I have already written fifteen and I could write many more without any problem.

Each short story takes me a few hours to write.

All this to tell you that it's not the same thing to start writing an e-book or a whole series of e-books.

I'll tell you why just a little further...

So if you have decided to treat yourself or to do like some of your acquaintances who have already been there and to write just one and only time, just to say that it is not only the others who can doing so, writing an e-book shouldn't be too much of a problem. Though...

On the other hand, if you really want to embark on the adventure of the e-book and you seriously intend to write a certain number of them, think carefully about your intentions and try to project yourself forward.

What are you going to do after writing your first e-book ?...

Do you have enough material to write more?...

Do you think they will be attractive enough to interest readers?...

Because quite frankly, writing and publishing e-books, just for the pleasure of writing and publishing them is not enough.

When you start writing and publishing e-books, it's to reap the rewards.

Fruit in the form of copyright, with every sale.

And this is where everything will get particularly complicated because expect nothing, but really nothing with the publication of only one, two, three or even four or five e-books.

Because between us, if nobody knows you, if nobody has heard of you, if you haven't appeared on TV or on the radio, how do you expect to collect royalties, knowing that you don't have no reader?...

The only way for you to succeed will be your productivity.

And who says productivity necessarily says quantity.

Except that it is not given to everyone to be able to write like that, just by snapping their fingers. And you will understand why.

*
* *

20

5 – Productivity and quality

A – Quality

▶ Concerning the quality, we saw it previously, it is absolutely necessary that you have real skills in a given field, before you start.

And above all, don't listen to all those hucksters who would have you believe that it's not a problem and that after a while you'll know more than the others.

They're just looking to sell their own lineups, often pumped left and right, knowing that for the most part, I mean most, they've never written anything very personal that they could claim authorship.

So they try to make you think it's easy, only it's not.

Besides, it's because there's a good reason for it.

If you don't know how to write even a simple article, forget the digital book, because writing an e-book requires the same skills and the same facilities as writing anything else.

And this is the reason why I try to develop new points, specific to e-books, since I assume that you have followed my previous training perfectly, which I remind you, are not only very progressive, but also very practical.

Indeed, they contain many concrete examples, not to mention a certain number of exercises which allow you to ensure constant progress.

B – Productivity

► Regarding productivity, this is where you will also have to ensure a maximum.

To start building a following and assuming you're writing quality eBooks on topics readers want, don't expect anything until you've published at least 20 of them.

It is the minimum of the minimum.

And again, don't think that everything will run like clockwork.

But I will tell you later, how to exploit this potential vein, because it is indeed a potential vein.

For the moment, we are not there yet, so let's get back to our sheep...

Because in fact, there is a small problem.

How to write at least twenty books on a well-targeted subject?

Unless you know it well, master it well, understand all its contours, master its ins and outs, it will be purely mission impossible.

And this is precisely the reason why I previously warned you about this notion of area of expertise.

Because make no mistake about it.

If all you're doing is saddening platitudes hoping to conquer, if not the heart, the purses of your readers, don't even think about it and don't embark on a path strewn with pitfalls and lost in advance.

To interest readers, you have to do no more and no less, do what I told you, namely: deliver anecdotes, entrust certain little manufacturing secrets, tell their origin and their history, all these very personal things of which you alone and nobody else got the scoop.

Readers want effective and original content that not only meets their needs, but also brings them that element of mystery that they seek through writing.

So as long as it's yours.

*

*   *

6 – Example

A – General area

For example, you have a job but it turns out that cooking is your hobby, your pastime and you know how to do it.

In this case, you will probably have no difficulty in writing on the subject and feeding it regularly, so much so that you will very quickly be in your twenty books, which, let us remember, are the minimum required to be able to derive some benefit from it.

On the other hand, if you know absolutely nothing about it and your only skill is cooking a soft-boiled egg, you can imagine the complication to come, as far as writing about twenty books on the subject !

All this to tell you not to jump in blindly.

So how to do ?...

After having detected your domain of competence, and assuming that it is indeed a real domain of competence, you will list on a sheet or an Excel table, all the sub-domains on which you will feel capable of writing.

B – Create a subdomain

Let's go back to the kitchen example.

We understand that this is not your job, but you have enough experience and practice to be able to assert certain skills in this area.

From there, you could decline on a lot of subjects in their own right, inherent to cooking in general.

When the subjects are many and varied, this is where you give yourself the best chance of being able to produce, produce again, again and again!

In fact, the kitchen is an endless chain with unlimited possibilities.

Rather judge :

The cuisine of all the countries of the world

The different kinds of cuisine cooking and diets

· Stewed dishes

· Dishes in sauce

· Baked dishes

· Cooking utensils

The art and manner at the table

Culinary principles

And so on, and the best !

Moreover, it is not by chance that in booksellers and newsagents, there are always many books related to cooking.

This is a subject that interests many people, proof of which is all the TV shows on a very large number of channels.

So, you list all these sub-domains on your sheet or on your Excel table and from there, you make new sub-domains.

C – Establish a sub-subdomain

For example, if you take the cuisine of all the countries of the world as a subdomain, you could have French cuisine, Italian cuisine, Chinese cuisine, Indian cuisine, etc.

As many subdomains as countries.

Did you get the point ?

From a **general area**, cooking, you have broken down into **sub-areas** (the cuisine of all the countries of the world, the different kinds of cuisine, cooking and diets, stews, dishes in sauce, oven dishes, cooking utensils, art and table manners, culinary principles, etc.)

From a **particular sub-domain**, for example, world cuisine, you have declined as many sub-domains as it is possible to imagine (French cuisine, Italian cuisine, Chinese cuisine, Indian cuisine, etc.)

Now, your range of possibilities has widened considerably and at this stage, you are sure and certain of being able to imagine a collection of at least fifty books.

But it is not finished !

From one of these subdomains, it is still possible to go into even more detail.

For example, if you take French cuisine as a subdomain, nothing prevents you from offering themes and categories specific to French cuisine and traditions only.

Same thing for the sub-domain Italian cuisine or Chinese or Indian cuisine, etc.

Your possibilities of writing thus become almost infinite.

D – Feeding the collection

And there, it is great happiness! Because you will be able to feed and enrich your collection with one e-book per week, once you have gotten used to it and the rhythm.

One digital book per week amounts to 52 e-books over a year !

And there, you may say to yourself that the trick is done and that's all that's left to do.

Except that...

I'm not here to tell you nonsense or to dangle untenable promises.

Why am I saying this ?...

Quite simply because in many training courses, it is said that all you have to do is write an e-book and after that, everything runs on its own and without doing anything !

Nothing is more false than this untruth.

On the one hand, it will never roll by itself and on the other hand, an e-book lost among millions and millions of other e-books is like looking for a needle in a haystack.

So you may be going to tell me, yes, but here, I wrote 52 and it's still not nothing.

It's true that 52 books in digital format, it's starting to count...

It's true that you will have invested yourself to get there.

It is true that it is a real personal work...

Except that to make this work profitable, it will be necessary to put actions in place.

Commercial actions, marketing actions, advertising actions.

But just before tackling these themes, which will be the subject of a later and completely separate training course, based on sales, let's quickly stop on the one hand, on the ideal number of pages for an e-book is taken seriously and on the other hand, on its selling price.

*

*   *

7 – The number of pages

The number of pages is another very important aspect.

Let's not forget that this is a book that you are going to present in digital version, therefore e-book format, and that your readers are waiting for solutions to their problems.

In our present case and for the example, we took the theme of the kitchen.

This being the case and whatever the themes or subjects, there is no rule in the matter.

This means that you can find e-books of ten pages and others of a hundred or even more.

So what to do ?

It's just a matter of common sense.

If you claim to have skills in a particular subject, you must give readers not only the impression but the certainty that with you, they will learn things they do not know.

And without getting into the game of filling in lines, filling in the blanks, a serious book on a serious subject cannot be treated in a few pages.

So try to situate yourself in several dozen pages of books, while respecting the quality of your content.

Several dozen pages means about fifty or more.

As a general rule, when dealing with a very specific topic, this will usually suffice.

But it remains an average and who says average
says a little more or a little less.

*

*   *

8 – The sale price

The selling price is what will determine your success.

Provided of course, that you have implemented all the actions quickly mentioned above (commercial actions, marketing actions, advertising actions) because without them, no one will know who you are and what you do.

The sale price therefore assumes that following all your actions, a certain number of potential readers have been made aware of your works.

The sale price also assumes that they've taken a closer look at your particular e-book they're interested in.

So they are ready to buy it.

Simply what is the ideal sale price, the one that would not risk putting them off ?

■ Because the difference between an e-book and a paper book is the manufacturing cost.

As much as the cost of making an e-book can be zero (if you did everything yourself from scratch and didn't use any paid apps), so much the cost of making a paper book will weigh on its selling price.

For a paper book, it is necessary to count, according to the number of copies printed, between 15% (for very large quantities greater than 50,000 copies) and 25% or even 35% (in print to order as is the case at Amazon POD, which means Print on Demand or print on demand)

That's one thing.

■ Next, shipping costs must be taken into account.

For an e-book, they are zero. (Always on condition that you take care of it yourself and with free applications)

For a paper book, they will represent up to 30% of the sale price.

■ And then finally the margin of the editor.

For an e-book, if you take care of everything and if you use free applications, your margin will be almost 100% since you will provide all the functions at the same time.

That is to say author, designer, marketer, advertiser, seller and distributor.

For a paper book, the publisher will leave you only 5% copyright when you start, going up to 10% when you are well known and you are able to exceed fifty thousand sales for a book and even more, up to 15% sometimes, for an essential author capable of ensuring sales of well over a hundred thousand copies for each novelty.

Note that very few authors in France can boast of such percentages...

All that to say what ?

Above all, don't be greedy, because by doing it well, by carrying out all the actions as appropriate, you will very much make up for it on the quantity.

Clearly, it is better to market your e-books at the price of a few euros each rather than looking for the jackpot, trying to sell them at an exorbitant price.

Let's take an example.

You have written 52 e-books, thanks to your knowledge, your experience and your imagination, on the subject of cooking.

They are all very personal works, in the sense that you have neither pumped right or left, nor have you plagiarized.

You have put in place all the actions likely to make you known and to make known all your works.

Imagine that you sell every day to all of your readers, even just one digital book per day, at the price of one euro each.

This gives 52 euros which comes back to you in full, since you will have set up to do this, only free applications.

Either 1,560 euros per month, or 18,720 euros over a year.

It will have required 52 weeks of effort for you to then build up an annual pension of 18,720 euros !

That's just for example with a selling price of one euro.

So imagine what it could look like with a higher selling price.

Two euros... Three euros...

Come on, it's up to you !

*

* *

Conclusion

You now have all the elements to start writing your future e-books.

Above all, follow the steps carefully and do not skip any.

Take the time necessary to carry out your research in order to gather the maximum of information likely to interest all your readers.

Do not hesitate to ask for help from anyone who can help you. Whether it's your family, your friends or all the relationships that can help you move forward in your journey.

Because even if writing is a work that is practiced alone, the ideas are often found in all the stakeholders when they find an interest likely to make things move forward.

*

* *

But before we leave, here are some particularly useful bonuses that I invite you to read carefully.

The first three are devoted to the distribution of your works. For this, I show you different tracks and I tell you how to go about it.

The fourth is devoted to the mind, more precisely to the "Mind Set". This bonus is very important because it is the basis of everything. On the one hand, it's about your ability to put in the work and on the other hand, it's about hanging on to your work. Because yes, even if writing is a

34

pleasure, the fact remains that nothing will be done by simply snapping your fingers.

The fifth is dedicated to reading work and you will realize how much it is not as simple as it seems.

The sixth is devoted to the meaning of words. This bonus is extremely important because you must certainly suspect it, each word can hold many surprises.

The seventh finally, is full of common sense and precisely, it can also serve you. Matter of common sense !

*

* *

Bonus 1

The book fairs

Do you like direct contact ?

Do you like approaching people ?

Do you like to exchange your points of view ?

So think about book fairs.

This can be a great way for you, not only to make yourself known, but also to sell some of your books.

There are many book fairs in France and no doubt there are some not far from where you live.

To find out, I invite you to consult the map of book fairs in France on the internet, as well as the annual calendar of all events. You will find there all the indications and all the information for the useful contacts.

In the same spirit, I also recommend that you take a look at the guide to book festivals, always full of good ideas.

It is best to register for several book fairs, preferably within a close or relatively close geographical radius, in order to facilitate your travels.

You will realize with use that it will be much more practical for you !

That said, nothing prevents you from participating in trade fairs that may be further away, but in larger cities.

As a general rule, registration is chargeable, with some exceptions.

On the other hand, it is not expensive and therefore very accessible.

There are even salons that offer lunch to their exhibiting writers. Nice no ?...

For climatic reasons, most fairs are held in a hall, the party room or any other multipurpose room.

In summer, in some areas, you can find them in the middle of the street or in a market place.

Equipment

In addition to your books, remember to bring the following accessories : a tablecloth to cover the table that will have been assigned to you, a support to affix a small A4 poster (21cm x 29.7cm), writing materials, visits in bookmark format, without forgetting to eat and drink.

Also plan a small wheeled trolley to lug all your equipment, just to avoid hurting your back.

Because a book fair lasts for one or several whole days and inevitably, you have to think of everything !

How it works

Well it's very simple.

You arrive at the agreed time, preferably in advance and you go to see the organizer who will tell you your location.

You haven't forgotten the famous tablecloth I told you about ?... So much the better because it's a good thing.

On the one hand, to brighten up and personalize your table and on the other hand, to hide anything that may be under the table.

That is to say your stock of books and everything that will be useful to you throughout the day.

Once your installation is done (usually it only takes a few minutes) walk through all the aisles, on the one hand to see which authors are exhibiting and on the other hand, to get to know them.

Some are regulars and inevitably, they can provide you with valuable information.

For example on the frequentation of the show, on the strokes of the flock and on the off-peak periods, etc.

You'll also learn which salons to go to and which ones aren't much going on.

Advertisement

Notify all your networks of your participation in your various shows.

Ask all your friends to relay and broadcast as much as possible.

If the organizers have planned something special or particular, such as a guide or newsletter, send them what is called in the jargon "a paper", i.e. a short presentation note on your production, so that she can be there.

Advertising is something very important and should not be taken lightly.

Proof of this is that if very large, world-famous brands continue to advertise regularly, it is probably not by chance.

Simply everything is a question of financial means. Even though in your mind it may seem ridiculous in terms of budget, it will always result in something in terms of payoff.

Your role at the show

Everyone will have their own strategy and that's normal, insofar as it will depend on your temperament and your way of seeing things.

What you need to know is that if you don't move, you're less likely to approach a potential reader than if you make an effort to do so.

So my advice is to make sure you get noticed, either by cleverly calling out to visitors, or by appropriate gestures or whatever comes to mind, as long as it is natural and never rude.

Because if you don't move, that is to say, you stay planted all day in your chair and behind your table, I'm not saying that it won't work, but what I'm saying is that you will deprive you of some possibilities of contact and therefore of sales.

However, the purpose of a book fair is, on the one hand, to make you known and, on the other hand, to sell.

Trade show strategy

There are writers who regularly participate in fairs, sometimes for many years.

By dint of frequenting them, they manage to create a kind of local clientele, made up of loyal and unconditional, to ultimately make some interesting sales, enough to put a little butter in the spinach at the end of the day.

So do not neglect this aspect and avoid making a sword in the water.

Participating in a book fair is a kind of achievement for a writer.

We are no longer at work.

We are having fun.

The pleasure of meeting his readers.

The pleasure of exchanging with them.

The pleasure of dedicating his work to them.

The more you make this pleasure attractive and communicative, the more successful you will be.

Important

Write down all your contacts.

Both those who have bought and those who have not.

As soon as you return, thank them all by sending them an email and attaching the cover of your publications.

Also specify the next trade fairs you plan to attend as this could give ideas...

In addition, do not forget to send them a little message of sympathy, during each important event, such as the end of year celebrations, an anniversary date, etc.

People are extremely sensitive to all these little attentions which necessarily make them very happy.

So don't deprive yourself of it because in the long run, it always ends up paying off !

How much can it bring ?

This is **THE** famous question !

How much does it pay ?...

There is no general rule, but know that your sales will depend above all on the organization of the show, the advertising put in place to make it known and the number of visitors.

It is very likely that for a given city, you will not have the same results during your first or during your third fair.

Quite simply because at the start, people don't know you.

On the other hand, by frequenting them regularly, you will see that sales will be made.

Moreover, it is not by chance that we find ourselves in the same place and every year, among fellow writers.

But for all this to work, you absolutely have to like direct contact, like approaching people and like exchanging points of view.

*

* *

Bonus 2

Signing sessions

Do you like direct contact ?

Do you like approaching people ?

Do you like to exchange points of view ?

Contrary to what one might think, signing sessions are not only reserved for well-known writers, those who appear on TV or who are heard on the radio.

In fact, it is very simple.

And it's free for you.

So all profit if it works!

First of all, you have to go see the booksellers to present your work to them and tell them about yourself, what you do and your way of seeing things.

You should know that there are bookstores and even large points of sale dedicated to stationery and books, which regularly organize meetings between the author and the public.

Others, however, do not.

It may be because the places are not suitable (most often a question of space) or more simply, because no one has thought of it. Like what...

So it will be up to you to value yourself, to put yourself forward, so as to obtain this long-awaited moment, that of meeting your future readers.

To find the signs, just look for them in your city or in any case, not too far from your place of residence.

How it works

You will see, it is remarkably simple.

Once you arrive at the merchant, you sit in the place that will have been reserved for you.

In general, when booksellers regularly practice these meetings between the author and the public, they always have a place reserved, most often sufficiently comfortable and easy to access.

However, do not hesitate to bring your personal point of view, if you see possible improvements.

It goes without saying that you arrive early enough to be ready in the best possible conditions.

And there is more than !...

Advertisement

Notify all your networks of your participation in your various signatures.

Ask all your friends to relay and broadcast as much as possible.

If the person in charge of the bookstore or the store has planned something special or particular, such as a guide or newsletter, pass him what is called in the jargon "a paper", i.e. a short note of presentation on your production, so that it can appear there.

Advertising is something very important and should not be taken lightly.

Proof of this is that if very large, world-famous brands continue to advertise regularly, it is probably not by chance.

Simply everything is a question of financial means.

Even though in your mind it may seem ridiculous in terms of budget, it will always result in something in terms of payoff.

Your role

Since the dedication goes through the purchase of your book, either you are known and this will necessarily happen automatically, or you are not and it will be up to you to convince your future readers.

In this context, there are not thirty-six solutions.

Either you don't move and you just wait for things to happen on their own, which is a possibility, or you move.

That's what I recommend to you.

This is why I reminded you in the preamble that you have to like contact with people, that you have to know how to approach them and that it is essential to exchange with them.

Because in reality, if no one knows you yet and for good reason, what could possibly make people want to read you?...

As much as the fact of writing is in no way a commercial action, the fact of selling it is a commercial strategy prepared in advance and well established afterwards.

So don't stay put and hopefully something will happen because in most cases, nothing will happen.

You have to provoke chance and for that, it's up to you to take your destiny into your own hands.

Strategy

Certain writers, when they are known, manage to sell more than three hundred books in half a day.

Everything is perfectly run and carefully timed.

No time to waste !

As far as you are concerned, the goal is to get people to know you and buy your book.

In the same way as at a book fair, you will have to showcase yourself, communicate, seduce, show empathy towards your audience and all that, as naturally as possible.

Suffice to say that the first time, it will not be won in advance but you will see, you get used to it very quickly!

For a writer, having a book signing is like a sort of culmination.

It's not work.

It's just fun.

The pleasure of meeting his readers.

The pleasure of exchanging with them.

The pleasure of dedicating his work to them.

The more you make this pleasure attractive and communicative, the more success you will have.

Important

It will not be possible for you to write down all your contacts, unless there are not many people and you have plenty of time to discuss the fat with your interlocutor.

On the other hand, plan several posters, in A3 format intended to be stuck on the window and in A4 format intended to be affixed in plain view on your work table.

On the poster, there will be your photo on the one hand and the cover photo of your book on the other.

People need to know who you are and be able to recognize you afterwards.

Also plan, if possible for you, a stock of bookmarks with the cover of your book as well as your e-mail address and do not hesitate to distribute them intensively.

How much can it bring ?

This is **THE** famous question !

How much does it pay ?...

There is no general rule but know that your sales will depend above all on the organization of this moment of dedications, the advertising put in place to make it known and the number of visitors.

But know that if the sale of a book brings you five euros for example, just with ten books, you will have already pocketed nearly fifty euros.

So imagine scheduling two book signings a week.

I'll let you do the math.

*

*   *

Bonus 3

Printing your book

Participating in book fairs or book signings is one thing, but selling your books is another.

Because for that, you need to have material to present to the public.

And what is this material ?...

It's simply the paperback, with real paper pages and a beautiful four-color cover.

However.

We all know that launching mass production can be very expensive and if there is no sale at the end, it will not only be a waste of time but also a lot of money wasted.

So I am going to suggest two publishing houses that may be of interest to you in case you wish to participate in book fairs or signing sessions.

Because in these cases, and unlike digital books (e-book), your reader will have to be able to obtain your book in paper version.

To do this, you need to find a publisher that prints books individually.

Apart from Amazon with its Print On Demand system, there are a number of them on the market, which you can easily find by searching on Google.

For your information, I will cite two of them.

I've never worked with these two houses but for all that, I've heard good things about them and that's why I take the liberty of talking about them. So in alphabetical order.

Book on demand : it is a house that is already well established and which will allow you, for a relatively modest price, to print your book.

Editions du Net : it is also a well-established house and which will also allow you to print your book, for a relatively modest cost.

Without going into details (for that, you just have to go to the BOD website - book on demand - or to the Editions du Net website) let's say that you will have all the help and assistance to format your work, calculate its selling price and determine your copyright.

Apart from these two houses that I have just mentioned, there are many, so do not limit your research and do not hesitate to explore others in case you deem it useful.

Not only will they allow you to publish your manuscript in digital form (ebook), but above all, they will give you the opportunity to present your novel at your favorite events, whether at a book fair or at a Book signing.

Because between us, can you imagine for a single moment, participating in literary fairs, without the public even being able to obtain your work?

During a book fair and even more so during a signing session, readers want paper books and not digital books.

That's the whole point of this kind of event, where you can meet your favorite author in the flesh, where you can chat with him and where you can get a dedication.

So unless you succeed in winning a publishing contract in good and due form, by a serious publishing house which would take all the costs of printing, distribution and advertising at its expense, the only way to achieve this is is the single print.

Once the terms of an agreement have been finalized with a publishing house producing single prints, you will only need to order a certain quantity for your personal needs, so that you always have a personal stock on hand.

So that for your future fairs, you do not arrive empty-handed and that you can respond to all requests.

*

*   *

Bonus 4

The mindset

In this bonus, I would like to mention a characteristic essential to any writer, whether known or not.

Because that goes for everyone.

If writing is accessible to everyone, the fact remains that to complete a book and this is precisely the case for a biography, you will have to show a certain temperament.

More precisely, of a certain strength of character.

This means that you will have to be able to resist all the usual frustrations and blockages.

*

* *

In fact, what will make you progress is what the Anglo-Saxons call the mind set, that is to say the state of mind.

The mind set is the strength of the spirit, the strength of character, the strength to want, the strength to move forward.

It is both a will to succeed, a mad and ardent desire, a feeling of power, a total absence of renunciation.

It is perseverance.

It is stubbornness.

It's "we don't give up !" »

That's all the mind set.

Basically, the difference between the one who has the mind set and the one who doesn't, is this desire not to let go.

When you have the mind set you don't give up.

Absolutely nothing.

Moreover, in writing as in many other areas, you must not give up.

*

*　*

In fact, writing is an activity full of pitfalls.

And inevitably, it will never be a very long calm river, so get ready for a real obstacle course with all its procession of traps and pitfalls.

Sometimes it's hard not to let go, to give up along the way, because of ideas that don't come, unless you don't know how to line them up, put them in place, so that after a some time, we are always at a standstill with this feeling that it's too hard, too complicated and that it won't do it!

So let's examine the following presentation, to understand the logical and natural evolution of a complete course in writing.

There is the past.

There is the present.

There is the future.

The past represents the sum of accumulated experiences.

They are the ones that will allow you to create a style, a feather as we say in the jargon and to lead your boat where you want to.

The future represents all the work that you will still have to accomplish to finalize your work.

The rest flows from source and it is obvious, because it is all your past actions which will determine your present.

And it is precisely this present that will allow you to project yourself into the future.

So the question : how do you value your past ?

Quite simply by being in tune with the perception of your work accomplished and with the energy that you will have to deploy to achieve your goals, ie the finality of your action.

*
* *

It is quite obvious that all your paths, at some point, will cross and that there is no absolute truth to arrive at the ideal situation.

And what is this ideal situation ?

It is simply when you will gradually become the perfect author, the ideal writer, the one capable of generating a million and more copies sold. Who knows ?...

All this will be guided by your brain, which is the common denominator of any initiative, the one that will propel you into action.

Because you have to know that when you're writing, you're constantly thinking.

It is your thinking that will guide you and that will play a decisive role, because without a perfectly reasoned and perfectly considered reflection, there can be no well-founded and winning action, in the medium and even less in the long term.

As much in the short term and with a little inspiration, you can get started without really knowing where you are going, in the long term you will not be able to without some experience, except that this experience, you will have to appropriate it.

And you will see that it will not be as easy as some would like us to suppose.

Indeed, I regularly see all kinds of training promising you to write a book in a few days (if not a few hours) then put it online to earn more or less substantial income.

Basically, we are offered two avenues.

One is to write and sell an e-book and the other is to write and sell a novel.

For the e-book, according to some authors, all you need to do is :

- choose the right subject...

- list people's problems...

- answer their problem...

- analyze statistics...

- build the plan of your e-book...

- create the appropriate structure...

- rephrase the titles...

Etc.

In fact, these are only generalities and very smart one who can write his first e-book by following such banalities and even more to sell it !

For the novel, it is not much better, since according to some authors, here is how it should be done:

- select inspiring themes...

- establish a plot of the story...

- build a detailed scenario...

- Supervise the construction of the characters...

- master the French language...

Etc.

More generalizations that will lead absolutely nowhere, I can guarantee you that, because no successful writer proceeds like that.

Besides, if this kind of recipe could work, no one would have any more problems with the famous blank page, you know, this desperately empty page that we spend hours contemplating, waiting for it to happen.

That being said, I can guarantee you that by following the advice of these people who haven't written much except to copy / paste and well it's not complicated, you will not be able to Nothing !

Know rather that writing is a real obstacle course. In this respect, you will have to thwart many pitfalls so as not to fall into crossroads and find certain tips to move forward in your writing project.

And this is precisely where you will have to know how to channel all your energy and all your attention, having a solid mind, foolproof, so that you can progress in your project until it is finalized.

And without this strength of character, without this very particular and oh so determining state of mind, without this famous mind set, you will never be able to succeed.

But I will tell you later how to do it and especially how to cultivate it. And you will see that from there, everything will be allowed to you !

*

*   *

Bonus 5

Reading work

Reading work, not proofreading work.

While the proofreading job is extremely important, because that's where you can pick up on anything that's wrong, because that's where you can make any necessary improvements, the reading job is no less important.

So what is a reading assignment ?

Reading for a writer is like doing scales for a pianist, or practicing free-kicks for a footballer.

In each specialty, regular training is required.

And that goes for all areas.

Writing is no exception to the rule and to progress you will have to read and read again. This is exactly the work of reading!

*
*   *

While the proofreading job is extremely important, because that's where you can pick up on anything that's wrong, because that's where you can make any necessary improvements, the reading job is no less important.

So what is a reading assignment?

Reading for a writer is like doing scales for a pianist, or practicing free-kicks for a footballer.

In each specialty, regular training is required.

And that goes for all areas.

Writing is no exception to the rule and to progress you will have to read and read again. This is exactly the work of reading!

*
*   *

Bonus 6

The meaning of words

In this bonus, I will address a very important point, namely the meaning of words or if you prefer, their meaning.

According to some, the French language is made up of about thirty thousand common words.

Listening to others, there would be dictionaries that could even bring together a hundred thousand.

Except that there is no work that does not specifically deal with this subject and that from there, all the hypotheses are open.

What is certain is that the French language is rich enough for you to never run out of words.

What is also certain is that it is not possible to know them all.

Especially since the language is constantly evolving and each year new ones appear.

What we can say, and almost without being too wrong, is that a sixth-grade student should know between three to five thousand, assuming that the school curriculum has been followed perfectly.

But knowing does not mean using on a daily basis.

Because in practice, the active vocabulary of most people will revolve around two or three thousand words, knowing that they will understand twice as many.

Here, take Victor Hugo, a great writer among the greats.

It seems that his active vocabulary, that is to say the words practiced on a daily basis, numbered no less than five thousand words.

But that's not all.

It seems that out of all his works, he would have used nearly twenty thousand.

All this to tell you what?

First, is not Victor Hugo who wants.

Second, don't try to misuse words.

In fact, that's what I've been trying to explain to you from the beginning.

Above all, do not complicate your life, under the pretext of trying to impress the gallery by using words that you did not know before and that you discovered by chance, but stay in simplicity and in your field of knowledge.

In particular, for example, I never use words that I do not know and I will never look for improbable synonyms, which no one will have heard of, barring an exception that confirms the rule.

For example, if I say **peu me chaut,** does that speak to you ?...

Another example, if I speak to you about **un parangon de vertu** does that cause you ?...

The word **dais**, you know ?...

Languide, have you ever come across this word ?

Une raucité, have you ever heard of it ?...

Do you know what **une branlette** is ?... But not the one you're thinking of !

Do you know what **une anatidaephobie** means ?...

Or **un vinculum** ?...

Good.

We are not going to do them all because on the one hand, there are so many that it will take us several days and on the other hand, it will absolutely not make you progress.

Why am I telling you this ?

Quite simply because they must be used sparingly and in a very specific context.

Always write according to your target and above all do not try to use learned words, pompous words or even words that have fallen into disuse.

Reading should above all be fun.

But how do you want to maintain this pleasure if you have to constantly look for the meaning of a word, an adjective, or even a noun ?...

In a nutshell, you have to make the reader want to turn the pages and not make the effort to go from one dictionary to another.

Come on, here is the meaning of these famous words, which many people do not know.

Peu me chaut comes from the verb chaloir. It means I don't care.

Un parangon de vertu is a model of virtue.

Un dais is a structure that can be made of wood or fabric and that extends above an altar, a pulpit or a bed.

Languide taken in the literary sense, means *Une raucité* languishing, languorous.

Une raucité is the character of what is hoarse. The voice has lost its hoarseness.

Une branlette is a fishing technique. It's all in the movement. Like what !...

Une anatidaephobie is simply the fear of being observed by a duck, anywhere in the world. (Surprising isn't it?)

Un vinculum is the fraction bar in a division.

Bonus 7

A very important reminder

In fact, this bonus is just a reminder.

But a reminder so important that I had to tell you about it one last time.

Because soon, this training will end.

And then it will be up to you.

It will be up to you to sit in front of your keyboard.

You see what I mean ?...

Not yet ?...

So here's another example that should get you started.

Attention ! Take your breath! Let's go !

Without honor but precarious, without freedom but provisional, until the discovery of the crime; only unstable, as for the poet the day before celebrated in all the salons, applauded in all the theaters of London, chased the next day from all the garnis without being able to find a pillow on which to rest his head, turning the millstone like Samson and saying like him: "The two sexes will die each on their side"; excluded even, except on days of great misfortune when the greatest number rallied around the victim, like the Jews around Dreyfus, from the sympathy – sometimes from society – of their fellow men, to whom they gave the disgust of seeing what 'they are, depicted in a mirror, which no longer flatters them, accuses all the flaws that they had not wanted to notice in themselves and which makes them understand that what they called their love (and to what, by playing on the word, they had, by social sense, annexed all that poetry, painting, music, chivalry, asceticism, could add to love) derives not from an ideal of beauty that 'they elected, but of an incurable disease; like the Jews again (except a few who only want to associate with those of their race, always have the ritual words and the consecrated jokes in their mouths) fleeing from each other, seeking those who are most opposed to them, who do not don't want them, forgiving their rebuffs, getting drunk on their complacency; but also brought together with their equals by the ostracism which strikes them, the opprobrium into which they have fallen, having ended by taking, by a persecution similar to that of Israel, the physical and moral characteristics of a race, sometimes beautiful, often dreadful, finding (despite all the mockery with which the one who, more mixed up, better assimilated to the opposing race, is relatively, in appearance, the least inverted, overwhelms the one who has remained more so), a relaxation in the frequentation of their similar, and even a support in their existence, so that, while denying that they are a race (whose name is the greatest insult), those who manage to hide that they are, they willingly unmask them, less to harm them, which they don't hate, than to apologize, and going to look like a doctor for appendicitis for the inversion even in history, having pleasure in recalling that Socrates was one of them , as the Israelites say of Jesus, without thinking that there were no abnormals when homosexuality was the norm, no anti-Christians before Christ, that reproach alone makes the crime, because he left only those who were refractory to all preaching, to all example, to all punishment, by virtue of an innate disposition so special that it is more repugnant to other men (although it can be accompanied high moral qualities) than certain vices which contradict it such as theft, cruelty, bad faith, better understood, therefore more excused by ordinary men; forming a Freemasonry much more extensive, more effective and less suspected than that of the lodges, because it rests on an identity of tastes, needs, habits, dangers, learning, knowledge, traffic, glossary, and in which the very members, who wish not to know each other, immediately recognize themselves by natural or conventional signs, involuntary or desired , who point out one of his fellows to the beggar in the great lord to whom he closes the door of his car, to the father in the fiancé of his daughter, to the one who had wanted to heal himself, to confess, who had to defend himself, in the doctor, in the priest, in the lawyer he went to find; all obliged to protect their secret, but having their share of a secret from others which the rest of humanity does not suspect and which makes the most implausible adventure novels seem true to them, because in this romantic life , anachronistic, the ambassador is a friend of the convict: the prince, with a certain freedom of bearing which gives an aristocratic education and which a trembling petty bourgeois would not have on leaving the duchess, goes to confer with apache; reprobate part of the human collectivity, but important part, suspected where it is not, displayed, insolent, unpunished where it is not divined; counting adherents everywhere, in the people, in the army, in the temple, in the galleys, on the throne; living finally, at least a great number, in the caressing and dangerous intimacy with the men of the other race, provoking them, playing with them to speak about his vice as if it were not his, game which is returned easy through the blindness or falsehood of others, a game that can go on for years until the day of the scandal when these tamers are devoured; until then forced to hide their lives, to divert their gaze from where they would like to fix themselves, to fix them on what they would like to turn away from, to change the gender of many adjectives in their vocabulary, social constraint, light with regard to the inner constraint that their vice, or what is improperly called so, no longer imposes on them with regard to others but to themselves, and in such a way that to themselves it does not appear to them to be a vice.

It is undoubtedly the longest sentence in the entire history of French literature.

It is taken from a work by Marcel Proust.

Did you manage to read it ?

Not sure...

This is to tell you not to get involved in endlessly long sentences.

At the risk of putting off all your readers.

Make short sentences !

Sentences of one or two lines, sometimes three and rarely more.

*
*   *